CAPE
AND THE ISLANDS

This edition published in 1993
by SMITHMARK Publishers Inc.,
16 East 32nd Street
New York, New York 10016.

SMITHMARK books are available for bulk purchase
for sales promotion and premium use. For details
write or telephone the Manager of Special Sales,
SMITHMARK Publishers Inc., 16 East 32nd Street,
New York, NY 10016. (212) 532-6600.

Produced by Brompton Books Corp.,
15 Sherwood Place,
Greenwich, CT 06830.

ISBN 0-8317-0804-2

Printed in Hong Hong

10 9 8 7 6 5 4 3 2 1

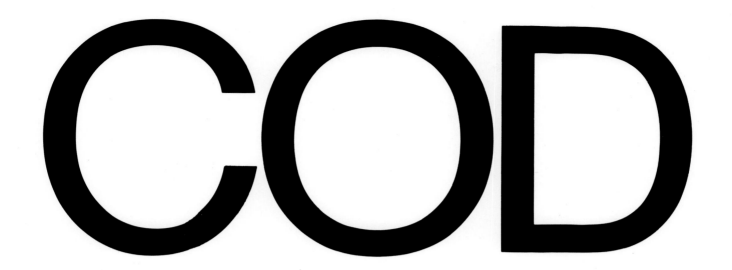

COD

TEXT   BARBARA PAULDING THRASHER

DESIGN   ADRIAN HODGKINS

SMITHMARK

To my brother and sister, Bob and Sue
Paulding, and their families, who keep the
Cape Cod home fires burning.

*3-6 The Nantucket waterfront, with its shingled
houses on stilts, presents an image of the
quintessential New England maritime town.*

PHOTO CREDITS

Catherine Karnow: 42-43, 56, 57 82, 85, 112, 114-115, 116,
  118, 119, 120, 121, 122-123,124,125,128.
New England Stock Photo: Roger Bickel:117; Brian L. Carr: 93;
  Bradford Glass: 3-6; Tom Hannon:102-103; Arnold J. Kaplan:
  41, 44, 58-59, 61, 75; Clark Linehan: 69; Gary Mirando: 105;
  Thomas H. Mitchell: 113; Lou Palmieri; 1, 38, 50 52, 53, 60,
  62-63, 65, 74, 76-77, 78, 79, 80, 81, 83, 84, 86-87, 88-89,
  90, 91, 92, 94-95, 96, 99; Kevin Shields: 66-67, 72-73; David
  R. Stevenson: 104.
Rainbow: Coco McCoy: 70; Dan McCoy: 36-37, 71, 101;
  Bonnie McGrath: 15, 22; Jim McGrath: 45; Hank Morgan:18,
  19, 97, 106-107, 108-109, 110, 126-127; Stephen F. Rose: 16-
  17, 20-21, 23, 24-25, 26-27, 28, 29, 30-31, 32, 33, 34, 35, 39,
  46, 47, 48-49, 51, 54-55, 68, 98,111.

INTRODUCTION

Cape Cod, described by Henry David Thoreau as the 'bare and bended arm of Massachusetts,' casts its sandy arc into the Atlantic, with its sister islands – Martha's Vineyard, Nantucket, and the Elizabeth Chain – to its south. Previously a peninsula, Cape Cod became an island in 1914 with the completion of the canal which bears its name. From the Upper Cape – the western, mainland side which borders (and straddles, in the case of Bourne) the canal – to the Outer Cape, which begins 35 miles east at the 'elbow' of Chatham and continues north for an equal distance, the average width of Cape Cod is six miles. When on the Cape you are never far from the ocean and its concomitant beaches – Cape Cod Bay to the north, the chilly Atlantic to the east, and Nantucket Sound, Vineyard Sound and Buzzards Bay to the south – and it is the ocean that imbues Cape Cod with its unique character. In this respect the Cape has changed little from 1865, when Thoreau wrote, 'Everything told of the sea, even when we did not see its waste or hear its roar. For birds there were gulls, and for carts in the fields, boats turned bottom upward against houses, and sometimes the rib of a whale was woven into the fence by the roadside.'

The distinct geology of Cape Cod began to be formed about 20,000 years ago during the last Ice Age, when the mountainous Wisconsin Glacier, up to two miles thick in places, pushed its way south from Canada, stopped, then slowly receded. The glacier left massive deposits – or moraines – of sand and stones in its wake, creating the unique shapes of Cape Cod and the islands. The southern shores of the islands and Cape are the glacier's outwash plains, comprised of finer, sandier fragments than the spine of the Outer Cape. Blocks of ice abandoned by the glacier melted, leaving depressions that became fresh-water and salt-water ponds, bogs and valleys. Even today nature continues to tamper with Cape Cod's landscape, as currents sculpt the outer shoreline, moving sand northward to the Provincelands shore and sandbars.

Despite the sandy, gravelly soil, five native American tribes of the Wampanoag Federation thrived on the Cape. They lived here as early as 10,000 years ago, subsisting on farming, fishing, trapping and hunting. No one is sure when the first white men came. Some accounts credit Thorwald, the son of Eric the Red, with a visit in 1004. The first documented landing occurred in 1602, when Bartholomew Gosnold arrived at the southwestern shore from Falmouth, England. Gosnold gave Cape Cod its name after the abundant codfish he found in its waters. Two years later Samuel de Champlain landed in Barnstable and wrote a description of the natives' way of life. In 1614 John Smith, in pursuit of whales, arrived at the Cape. He drew one of the first maps. Soon after Smith's departure an incident occurred that marred the generally friendly relations between whites and native Americans. Captain Thomas Hunt kidnapped 24 natives – among them Squanto – to sell as slaves in Spain. Squanto made his way back to America, where he became a valuable friend of the Pilgrims.

After a long and anxious journey, the *Mayflower* landed in Provincetown on November 9, 1620. To formalize their new beginning and commit themselves to the new government they would establish, the Pilgrim men signed the Mayflower Compact. Their explorations of the Provincetown area lasted more than a month, during which time three of their group died and one – the first white child known to be born in New England, Peregrine White – was born. A stash of buried corn discovered by the Pilgrims provided them with life-giving seed to plant in the spring, by which time they had settled in Plymouth, though three Pilgrims later emigrated to Cape Cod. Provincetown's Pilgrim Monument and Pilgrim Bas Relief commemorates the *Mayflower*'s historic arrival.

As the Plymouth colony expanded and more Europeans arrived, colonists began to settle the westernmost area of Cape Cod – first Sandwich and Barnstable, then east to Yarmouth and Eastham. The Cape's salt marshes provided fodder for livestock, and fishing, of course, offered a good living. Early settlers maintained a strict code of behavior, reinforced by various painful and humiliating forms of punishment. The 'Curious Forms of Colonial Punishment' display at the Dennis Police Station, with its stocks, whipping post and pillories, serves as a reminder of those times.

As tensions between the new and old worlds increased, so did clashes between Tories and patriots, on Cape Cod and throughout New England. A resident of Barnstable, James Otis Jr., is credited with introducing the idea of American independence in 1761. When war did break out, the Cape contributed Continental Army recruits and provided shore watches. The British ship-of-war, the *Somerset*, sailed regularly in and out of Provincetown, but was wrecked at North Truro in November of 1778, with all 480 survivors captured. In 1779 Cape Codders repulsed a British attempt to invade Falmouth. When the war ended, Cape Cod went about business as usual, but with a new fervor. War would touch Cape Cod again briefly in each of the next two centuries: a British warship was repelled at Orleans in the War of 1812, and in 1918 a German submarine sank four barges and a tugboat three miles off Nauset Beach.

But before and between these two anomalies the culture and economy of Cape

Cod flourished. Tourism, fishing, salt works and farming supported a burgeoning population. The writings of Herman Melville, who was a seaman aboard a Nantucket whaling ship in the 1830s, and Henry David Thoreau, who made four trips to the Cape between 1849 and 1857, familiarized the nation with the landscape and inhabitants of Cape Cod and the islands. The first land boom occurred in 1871, with the Hyannis Land Company buying up 1000 acres. A train line bringing wealthy vacationers from Boston contributed to the Cape's growing reputation as a fashionable destination. The beauty, opportunities for solitude, and idiosyncratic nature of the people of Cape Cod attracted those who appreciate such things, and the first influx of artists – from Europe and from New York City's Greenwich Village – arrived at the turn of the century. Broadway and London actor Joseph Jefferson built a Victorian mansion in Bourne in 1889. Ten years later the Cape Cod School of Art was founded in Provincetown by impressionist painter Charles W Hawthorne. By 1916 the small but lively fishing village of Provincetown – with its many Portuguese and Cape Verdean inhabitants, and its inexpensive cost of living – harbored five art schools and a theater group called The Provincetown Players, which included the young playwright Eugene O'Neill.

The theater arts continued to flourish on the Cape with the coming of the Barnstable Comedy Club in 1922 (which later included novelist Kurt Vonnegut), the Cape Playhouse in Dennis in 1927, and the University Players Guild – precursor of today's Falmouth Playhouse – in 1928. Many actors and actresses who went on to Hollywood fame performed in these groups, including Bette Davis, Henry Fonda, Ethel Barrymore, Humphrey Bogart, James Cagney, Orson Welles and James Stewart. Provincetown remained one of the country's foremost artists' colonies for almost half a century, and has revived its reputation in recent years.

Working art studios and galleries abound, and the community's Fine Arts Work Center hosts, among others, John Cheever, Norman Mailer, John Irving, Robert Motherwell and Stanley Kunitz.

While the arts are an important aspect of Cape Cod's past and present, few would deny that most people who come here are attracted primarily by the sheer beauty, the beaches, and the chance to have fun. For the vacationer seeking to experience nature's grandeur, Cape Cod National Seashore, established in 1961, offers ample opportunity. Encompassing 27, 300 acres of the Outer Cape, the National Seashore stretches from Chatham to Provincetown. Marshland, sand cliffs and dunes frame magnificent white beaches that lie in sharp contrast to the deep blue waters of the Atlantic. The moors and wildflowers of Nantucket, the rolling farmland and red cliffs of Martha's Vineyard, the quiet solitude of the Elizabeth Islands, and the abundance of unspoiled beaches and parks of the Upper and Mid Cape all contribute to the wealth and diversity of Cape Cod's natural world.

This diversity is mirrored in other aspects of Cape Cod as well. The ethnic mix of its people, predominantly Yankee and Portuguese; the range of architecture, which includes the simple Cape Cod house, Greek Revival, Federal and Victorian styles; and the many venues for recreation, from fishing to souvenir shopping, boating to miniature golfing, and bicycling to bird watching, all contribute to Cape Cod's enormous appeal. And if you're one of the lucky ones who appreciate the still, clear water of a deep kettle pond, roses against silver-gray shingles, a colorful ground carpet of heather and beach plum punctuated by the spiky trunks of scrub pine and oak, an ocean sunset, making small talk on a fishing pier, or enjoying an outdoor concert on a warm summer night, you may just become a Cape Codder yourself!

THE UPPER CAPE

The Bourne and Sagamore bridges arch over the Cape Cod Canal, connecting the Upper Cape to the Massachusetts mainland. The Upper Cape – consisting of the towns of Sandwich, Bourne, Falmouth, and Mashpee – is the first area of Cape Cod glimpsed by most visitors. The steeply-arched bridges, reminiscent of Erector set contraptions, inspire a childlike excitement in the most seasoned traveller. Making the descent onto Cape Cod, it is easy to feel, and rightly so, that this is the beginning of an adventure.

The town of Sandwich, Cape Cod's oldest, consists of seven villages. Established as a trading post in 1627, Sandwich was settled 10 years later by pioneering families, and was incorporated in 1639. Many remnants of the past lend character to this beautiful old town, from 350-year-old saltbox cape houses and a working grist mill to stately sea captains' homes and summer mansions. Sandwich also offers a diversity of nature's pleasures, including the Sandwich Marsh, Sandwich Town Beach, Shawme-Crowell State Forest, and russet-colored cranberry bogs.

Extending southwest along the canal, the town of Bourne was once part of Sandwich. Its seven villages include Bournedale and Buzzards Bay on the Massachusetts mainland; Sagamore, which straddles the canal; Bourne Village, which boasts the Aptucxet Trading Post, where profits were used by the Pilgrims to repay London merchants who financed the *Mayflower*; and the beachside residential communities of Monument Beach, Pocasset and Cataumet. Much of Bourne still harbors the historic nineteenth-century factories, mills and wharves that supported the town's shipbuilding, manufacturing and fishing industries. In contrast, Bourne's villages along Buzzards Bay feature expansive stretches of sandy beach interrupted by picturesque harbors, marinas and lighthouses.

The eight villages of Falmouth, south of Bourne, accommodate 100,000 summer residents, more than triple its year-round population. From the bustling village of Woods Hole, best known as a ferry terminal to the islands and for the maritime research centers of its renowned Woods Hole Oceanographic Institute, to quiet and exclusive West Falmouth, with its beautiful harbor, the villages of Falmouth maintain distinctive characters.

East of Falmouth and south of Sandwich, the town of Mashpee embraces old and new worlds. The Wampanoag Indian Museum and Tribal Council Building of Mashpee Center, and the annual Indian Pow-wow, underscore the fact that Mashpee has long been home to the Massippee tribe of the Wampanoag Federation. Although it was established as a Plymouth colony in the late 1600s, and incorporated as a town in 1870, Mashpee's political history has been complicated by the struggle for land ownership. Today the old Mashpee remains unchanged in such protected areas as the 432 acres of marshes, pine woods and barrier beach of South Cape Beach State Park, while a newer Mashpee is represented in the modern amenities of the 2000-acre New Seabury resort complex.

This spirit of old and new pervades much of the Upper Cape, where rowdy nightspots and bustling harbors are never far from hilly farmland and quiet beaches rimmed with goldenrod, beach grass and dusty miller. But one thing about the Upper Cape remains unchanged – there is always much to discover.

15 Nobska Light, on Nobska Point just east of Woods Hole Harbor in Falmouth, shines its beacon for as many as 30,000 ships that pass here annually. Built in 1828, the fixed beacon can be seen for 15 miles at sea.

16-17 Bikers watch the sunset across Cape Cod Canal, framed by the Bourne Bridge. Built between 1909 and 1914, the Canal initially cost $16 million. The 17-mile-long, 540-feet-wide canal is bordered by scenic highways on both sides. The Bourne and Sagamore bridges, completed in 1935 to replace drawbridges, connect Cape Cod to the Massachusetts mainland.

18 The Sandwich Glass Museum displays colored glassware from the renowned Boston and Sandwich Glasswork Company, which operated from 1825 to 1888. The nation's largest early glass factories produced pressed lacy glass with a stippled background, and blown, cut and engraved glassware.

19 Neighbors enjoy a summer afternoon in the shade outside a colonial saltbox house in Sandwich. The oldest Cape Cod town (1637), Sandwich contains many examples of early Cape architecture.

20-21 Horse and rider canter along the beach in West Falmouth.

22 Considered the oldest house on Cape Cod
(1637), Sandwich's Hoxie House – owned in the
1800s by whaling captain Abraham Hoxie –
features thick timbers, a salt box roof and a
serene view of Shawme Lake.

23 The richly hued interior of the Hoxie House, with its colonial artifacts, makes the past seem comfortable and near at hand.

24-25 Graceful boats reflect in the placid water of Falmouth Harbor at dawn. Shipbuilding and whaling both played major roles in the town's nineteenth-century economy.

26-27 The Waquoit Congregational Church, established in 1848, adds a New England accent to the scenic drive along Route 28. Waquoit is a village of Falmouth, the town settled by Congregationalists and Quakers seeking reprieve from religious repression in Sandwich and Barnstable.

28 Visitors stroll the walkways at Heritage Plantation of Sandwich. With 76 acres of gardens and woodlands, historic collections of antique cars and military artifacts, and a beautiful old working carousel, Heritage Plantation attracts more than 100,000 visitors a year.

29 A fife and drum corps marches in the Veterans Day Parade at Otis Air Force Base. Otis is part of the 14,700-acre Massachusetts Military Reservation off Falmouth-Sandwich Road, located in the center of the Upper Cape.

30-31 Vacationers enjoy volleyball and sunbathing at Falmouth Heights Beach on Vineyard Sound. Falmouth, bordered by water on two sides, has the most coastline of any Cape town, with 14 harbors, 10 public beaches, and more than 30 ponds.

32 A Cape Codder scrubs down his boat on Monument Beach. A village of Bourne, Monument Beach combines seaside community and scenic beach near the Buzzards Bay shoreline.

33 Tuna fishermen out of Sandwich weigh their catch. As in many Cape Cod towns, fishing boats may be chartered out of Falmouth.

34 A beautiful and intricate kite, reminiscent of stained glass, is launched at Falmouth Heights. Kite-flying is a great way to spend an afternoon at the beach, listening to the cries of gulls and the waves breaking.

35 Children prepare to march in Falmouth's annual Hat Parade. Other notable events in Falmouth include the Barnstable County Fair, the Falmouth Road Race and the Christmas Parade.

36-37 An aerial view of Woods Hole, known for its world-famous Woods Hole Oceanographic Institute (WHOI). A center for oceanic research, the WHOI sent the expedition team that found the Titanic in 1986. The scientific community of Woods Hole also includes the Marine Fisheries Aquarium and the Marine Biological Laboratory.

38 Seaside dining in Woods Hole features fresh seafood, fresh air and a nautical view. Woods Hole Harbor provides ferry service to Martha's Vineyard and Nantucket.

39 Students aboard the Corwith Cramer *of the Woods Hole Marine Biological Laboratory take a hands-on six-week summer oceanography course.*

THE MID CAPE

'We often love to think now of the life of men on beaches, – at least in midsummer, when the weather is serene; their sunny lives on the sand, amid the beach-grass and the bayberries, their companion a cow, their wealth a jag of driftwood or a few beach-plums, and their music the surf and the peep of a beach-bird.' When Thoreau wrote this, except for the reference to the cow, he may have been describing summer at many of the Mid Cape's beautiful beaches today. For all the hustle and bustle of visitors vying for their place in the sun, there is more than enough beach here to go around. But the Mid Cape is much more than summer and beaches. Many of Cape Cod's year-round residents live here, and enjoy the changing faces of land and sea when the tourists have left and autumn touches the landscape. Though winter can be dreary, it is relatively mild, and spring seems to come early, coloring hillsides with crocuses and daffodils.

The 100 square miles of the Mid Cape are divided vertically into three towns – Barnstable, Yarmouth and Dennis – and each of these towns is comprised of villages. Barnstable, the Cape's largest town by far, is home to some 27,000 people. The most well-known of Barnstable's villages is the busy hub of the Cape, Hyannis. Named after the Indian chieftain Iyannough, Hyannis is located in Barnstable's southeast corner, on Lewis Bay. Not far from the Kennedy Compound, the John F Kennedy Memorial Park pays tribute to the American president who grew up on Cape Cod. With its many hotels, condominiums and restaurants, and its mall, airport, train depot and ferry terminal, Hyannis has grown up fast, and continues to live a colorful life.

Long before Barnstable became a mecca for the world-weary, it was heavily populated along the north shore by the Cummaquid, Mattakeese and Nobscusset tribes of the Wampanoag Indian Federation. Caring mainly to retain fishing and farming rights they sold what is now Hyannis, Hyannis Port, Centerville and Craigville to white settlers for 'twenty pounds and two small breeches.' Accompanying the Congregationalist minister John Lothrop, 22 followers settled in Barnstable's north shore in 1639. A farming and shore whaling subsistence shifted to off-shore whaling and fishing in the eighteenth century, though the local economy suffered from British blockades during the Revolutionary War. By the following century, many Mid Cape shipmasters made their fortune skippering the speedy American clipper ships, which carried cargo around the world. Several of their mansions still exist, among them Captain Rodney Baxter's Octagonal House in Hyannis, built in 1850.

As in other Mid Cape towns, Barnstable's busy, commercial areas are centered along the south shore. But such quiet, residential villages as Marstons Mills and Centerville remain as pastoral reminders of an earlier time.

East of Barnstable, fast-growing Yarmouth, with its five villages, also blends history and modern day living. From the northern village of Yarmouth Port, where legend holds that the Norseman Thorvald was killed by Indians while repairing his ship (hence Yarmouth's many Norse place names), to South Yarmouth's Smuggler's Beach, where colonists smuggled goods ashore to avoid British taxes, and rum runners landed liquor during Prohibition, Yarmouth has had a colorful past.

Once part of Yarmouth, Dennis to the east became its own town in 1793. The villages of Dennis lay claim to the Shiverick Shipyards, where clipper ships were built in the nineteenth century; the Cape Playhouse, which has entertained theatergoers since 1926 and the Scargo Lake and Tower, offering an 80-mile view from the Mid Cape's highest vantage point. Shaped by its past and by the tourism industries of today, the Dennis landscape – like that of the other Mid Cape towns – ranges from peaceful beaches and hilly farmland to bustling harbors, busy shopping areas, and streets lined with weathered cottages and white picket fences.

41 A slice of Cape Cod antiquity can be had at West Barnstable's Trading Company, one of Barnstable's dozens of folksy antique shops.

42-43 Although some Mid Cape beaches can get crowded, quiet beachfront can always be found along the ample shores. Swimming, contemplating the sea, napping under an umbrella, or digging in the sand can easily encompass an entire, timeless day.

44 A winter scene in Osterville exudes the
tranquil beauty that characterizes Cape Cod in
the off-season.

45 The Hyannis Lighthouse is decked out with
lights at Christmas time. The annual Hyannis
Festival of Light at the end of November features
the lighting of the village tree and other holiday
events to brighten winter nights.

46 Sailboat crews and their gear crowd into a
shuttle boat in Hyannis for the annual Figawi race.

47 Poetry in motion: a racing sailboat slices
through the waters of Nantucket Sound, heeling to
the wind.

48-49 Welcoming early spring, crocuses carpet the
front lawn of a colonial house in Barnstable.
Although the ocean moderates winters somewhat,
Cape Codders are just as happy as any New
Englander when spring arrives and the damp,
windy weather subsides.

50 Plant life well-adapted to sand and salt carpet the dunes and valleys of Barnstable's Sandy Neck, an eight-mile-long barrier beach that extends east along the Cape's northern shore into Cape Cod Bay.

51 Autumn foliage encircles Mill Pond in Marstons Mills, while swans feed in the placid water. In 1738 the first Marston arrived in the area that would become this quiet inland village of Barnstable, and ran the first of the village's many mills powered by Goodspeed's River.

52 A profusion of midsummer flowers spills through the post-and-rail fence at the Charles Hinckley House, a year-round bed and breakfast in the village of Barnstable.

53 Separate seating for those of diverse political views adds whimsy to the 1856 Country Store in Centerville, which sells everything from newspapers to penny candy.

54-55 Prepared for any weather, fishermen test their luck off the breakwater at South Yarmouth's Seagull Beach. One of the warmer, sandier beaches on the Cape's South Shore, Seagull Beach is popular with families.

56 Cape Cod's oldest inn, Old Yarmouth Inn was
the place, it is told, where Sam Black Bellamy and
a few of his friends were shanghaied onto a British
man-of-war. Bellamy and company killed the
officers, took over the ship and became pirates,
causing havoc on both sides of the Atlantic.

57 One of Yarmouth's 11 churches, this beautiful New England church reaches its spire into the dusk. Many Cape Cod churches have ancient cemeteries, where gravestones mark the places of the sea captains, millers, farmers and fishermen who shaped their community.

58-59 A walkway extends over the marsh at Yarmouth Port's Bass Hole, a scenic cove on Cape Cod Bay from which brilliant sunsets can be viewed.

60 Mums and pumpkins form an autumn still life at Toby Farm in Dennis, which offers fresh produce from one of the rural Cape's many family farms.

61 Lobster buoys and weathered shingles form a colorful mural on the side of a Mid Cape fishing shack. Fishing continues to offer a livelihood to seafaring Cape Codders.

62-63 A breakwater and sand dunes flank the inlet to Sesuit Harbor on Cape Cod Bay in East Dennis, sandwiched between Corporation Beach to the west and Cold Storage Beach to the east. The historic little village of East Dennis contains some very old and well kept colonial houses and sea captains' homes.

THE OUTER CAPE

That much of the Outer Cape remains undeveloped is partly the result of its remoteness, but also stems from the fact that some 27,000 acres of its land, with 30 miles of coastline, is part of the Cape Cod National Seashore. Land in six of the eight towns that comprise the Outer Cape is within the National Seashore, which ranges north from the Cape's 'elbow' at Chatham to the 'fist' at Provincetown.

The towns of the Outer Cape – Brewster, Harwich, Chatham, Orleans, Eastham, Wellfleet, Truro and Provincetown – share a rich and varied maritime heritage. Once part of Harwich, Brewster was settled in 1656 and incorporated as a town in 1803. Bounded on the north by Cape Cod Bay, Brewster maintained an economy through the nineteenth century centered on the great trading ships that ranged around the world. Much of Brewster's architecture – a mixture of Georgian, classic Greek Revival and Victorian houses, many with widow's walks – dates to the heyday of its many sea captains.

South of Brewster, the seven villages of Harwich are home to some 9500 residents, many of whom make their livelihoods in the tourism, fishing and cranberry business. Harwich is best known for its five protected harbors along the Nantucket Sound shoreline, and for its two-week Cranberry Festival, which includes fireworks, a parade and the Cranberry Ball.

East of Harwich, bounded on its other sides by Pleasant Bay, the Atlantic Ocean and Nantucket Sound, Chatham boasts 65 miles of waterfront. The upscale shops, restaurants and art galleries of its picturesque town center are just as much a part of Chatham's image as the mardi gras atmosphere at Aunt Lydia's Cove when fishing boats off-load their catches at the Chatham Fish Pier. The desolate beauty of Chatham's Monomoy Island, a nine-mile-long sand spit that juts south into Nantucket Sound, is rivaled by the spectacular ocean views along Chatham's Shore Road.

Chatham shares Pleasant Bay with Orleans to the north. Known as the business center of the Outer Cape, Orleans ranges from Pleasant Bay on the east – where it is said some of Captain Kidd's treasure is buried – to historic Rock Harbor on the west, where a British frigate was captured during the War of 1812.

The Cape narrows to three miles in Eastham, a town with some of the area's finest beaches, coves and ponds. From the marshside trails of the National Seashore's Salt Pond Visitor's Center, to the bayside First Encounter Beach, where an expedition led by Myles Standish first encountered Indians, there is much to discover in Eastham.

A leisurely pace is the order of the day in Wellfleet, north of Eastham. While the town has the feel of both an old fishing village and a summer arts colony, the land – protected by the Wellfleet Bay Wildlife Sanctuary, the National Seashore and Great Island – has the feel of a wilderness.

The moors, marshes and dunes of Wellfleet continue north through Truro, a rural, hilly town with scenic back roads and village settlements. From Truro's pretty Pamet Harbor on the bay, whaling and packet ships sailed forth, some never to return.

Located on the curled tip of Cape Cod, Provincetown is a seafaring village with an artistic flair. Both casual and sophisticated, downtown Provincetown combines a profusion of art galleries, wharves crowded with fishing fleets and touring boats, souvenir and craft shops, cafes, guest houses, restaurants and the ever-present sweet shops.

Provincetown is an amalgamation of all that is quintessentially the Outer Cape – beautiful beaches and rolling sand dunes, historic sites celebrating a colorful colonial and maritime history, bustling seaports, and a diverse population that finds common ground in the shared treasure of their land.

65 Wild roses and beach plum abound near the Wellfleet shore. Most of Wellfleet is located within the boundaries of the Cape Cod National Seashore. The integrity of Wellfleet's natural land is further ensured by the 700 acres of moors, marsh and forest located in the Wellfleet Bay Wildlife Sanctuary.

66-67 Located at the eastern end of Harding's Beach in Chatham, the Stage Harbor Lighthouse once guided ships into the harbor inlet from Nantucket Sound. The French explorer Samuel de Champlain anchored here in 1606, and engaged in a bloody battle with Indians at nearby Taylor's Neck.

70 Thompson's Clam Bar in downtown Harwich Port offers dockside dining on picturesque Wychmere Harbor.

71 Sailboats crowd a Harwich Port harbor on Nantucket Sound. Harwich Port's harbors – Wychmere and Saquatucket – are both manmade.

72-73 Tourists and locals mingle outside the Brewster Store, an authentic general store selling everything from crafts to coffee.

68 The Wee John III anchors in Chatham Harbor, protected from the Atlantic by the offshore island of South Beach.

69 The clear water and uncrowded expanse of a beach in Chatham beckon.

74 The weathered hull of a boat overlooks
Rock Harbor at Orleans. Although access to the
harbor is restricted by the tide, it is home to one
of the Cape's largest charter fishing fleets. At this
site during the War of 1812, the local militia
turned back the British, then captured the British
frigate Newcastle, which had gotten grounded in
offshore shallows.

75 Young's Fish Market, next to the marina at Rock Harbor, offers a seasonal variety of fresh fish and shellfish.

76-77 Beached catamarans at Pleasant Bay, a large cove shared by Chatham, Harwich and Orleans, await another day of skimming across the ocean. Pleasant Bay is protected from the Atlantic on the east by North Beach, a sandy peninsula that runs south from Orleans.

78 The Old Schoolhouse Museum in Eastham features the distinctive whale jawbone arch. Originally a one-room schoolhouse built in 1869, the museum houses artifacts from shipwrecks and the old school.

79 With its silver-gray shingles and wildflowers, the historic Knowles Doane house in Eastham offers a glimpse into Cape Cod's past.

80 Bikers pause to take in a scenic view of the Atlantic at Nauset Light Beach in Eastham, part of the Cape Cod National Seashore.

81 Eastham's Nauset Lighthouse sits atop a bluff over the Atlantic, where the 'Three Sisters' lights were lost to erosion.

82 Girls dig in the sand at Nauset Beach in East Orleans, one of Cape Cod's finest beaches. Site of many shipwrecks, Nauset Beach's most recent casualty was the Maltese freighter Eldia, *which washed ashore in a storm in 1984.*

83 A family wades at First Encounter Beach on Eastham's western bay side, the site of the first meeting between Indians and Mayflower *Pilgrims.*

84 Hiking trails and boardwalks through marshland and forest make exploring Wellfleet's wilderness fun.

85 Headquarters of Cape Cod National Seashore, the Marconi Station Area in South Wellfleet harbors remains of the original station from which the first wireless signal between the United States and Europe was transmitted, in 1903.

86-87 Beach houses in Truro offer the ideal setting for parties and family fun. With its miles of beaches, moors, cliffs and valleys, the rural town of Truro has a sparse year-round population of 2000.

88-89 The 255-foot Pilgrim Monument dominates the Provincetown skyline at sunset. This lively community at the very end of Cape Cod – with its art galleries, fishing fleets, tourist traps and swinging nightlife – offers a little bit of everything.

90 An old ship's figurehead mounted on a house in Provincetown gives testament to the town's seafaring past.

91 A fantastic mural on a Provincetown shopfront adds color to the town center along Commercial Street, where shopping takes a back seat to people-watching.

92 A Provincetown artist paints a garden scene.
Ever since the impressionist painter Charles W.
Hawthorne established the Cape Cod School of
Art here in 1899, Provincetown has been a
mecca for the arts.

93 Many visitors to Provincetown ride out to sea
on Whale Watch vessels to see the migrating
whales up close.

94-95 Diners enjoy a leisurely meal in one of
Provincetown's many outdoor cafes. In a town
where the population swells from 3000 to 30,000
in the height of the summer, cafes such as this
provide a welcome reprieve.

96 Fishermen work amidst a jumble of nets and
lines aboard fishing boats at Provincetown's Old
Pier.

97 In Provincetown's annual Blessing of the Fleet, decorated fishing boats process past MacMillan Wharf, where a bishop dispenses holy water and blessings for a safe and bountiful fishing season.

98 North of Provincetown's center, the Province
Lands are part of the Cape Cod National
Seashore. Miles of sand dunes and beaches
have changed little since Thoreau visited the area
more than a century ago.

99 A man surf fishes at sunset on Race Point
Beach north of Provincetown center.

THE ISLANDS

South of Cape Cod, Martha's Vineyard, the Elizabeth Islands and Nantucket share a rich maritime history. Although the islands host a thriving summer population, their beautiful and varied landscapes, historic architecture, and remoteness offer respite for the world-weary.

The English explorer Bartholomew Gosnold named Martha's Vineyard in 1602 after his daughter, and for the profusion of wild grapes growing on the island. Arriving in 1642, the Vineyard's first hardy settlers established themselves in what would become Edgartown, and 50 years later the island became part of Massachusetts. With fishing and whaling lore gleaned from the local Indians, islanders began to make their fortunes at sea, and the prosperous days continued – with a setback during the Revolutionary War, when the British destroyed the Vineyard's fishing fleet – until the demise of the whaling industry in the 1860s. The captains' mansions of Edgartown and Vineyard Haven hail from the whalers' heyday, and added glamor to the island's reputation as it became a resort community at the turn of the century. Farming and fishing continue to support some islanders, but the population of 10,000 also includes merchants, celebrities and statesmen. 'The Vineyard,' as it is known, contains several townships, from Vineyard Haven, Oak Bluffs and Edgartown on the busy 'Down Island' eastern side of the island, to West Tisbury, Chilmark and Gay Head on the western side. The island's unique landscape ranges from the white beaches, dunes, grasslands and bluffs of Chappaquiddick to the rocky farmlands, forests, quiet coves and ponds to the west.

From the towering red clay cliffs of Gay Head that comprise Martha's Vineyard's westernmost point, Cuttyhunk Island can be seen seven miles northwest. Part of the windswept Elizabeth Island chain, Cuttyhunk is the only of its islands fully open to the public. With 25 year-round residents, it is also the most populous. The Elizabeth chain – consisting of 16 small islands that reach southwest from Woods Hole – comprises the town of Gosnold. From the largest, Naushon, privately owned since 1842 and featuring idyllic Tarpaulin Cove, to Cuttyhunk, with many of its houses made from shipwrecks, the Elizabeth Islands are far removed from the madding crowd.

Midway in size between Martha's Vineyard and the Elizabeths, Nantucket shines its beacons from 30 miles south of Cape Cod. Much of the island's early American architecture dates from whaling days, and is preserved as a designated 'Old Historic District.' The Great Fire of 1846 – which destroyed the town's waterfront and business district – and the decline of the whaling industry sent Nantucket into an economic depression, in which it foundered for almost a century. But tourism brought a new prosperity in the 1950s, and by the 1960s much of the town was renovated and the marina was built. A walk along cobblestoned Main Street, lined with stately elms, brick buildings, old-time shops and captains' mansions, is like a stroll into the nineteenth century.

Protected from development, a quarter of Nantucket's land is owned by conservation groups. From the windswept barrier beach of Great Point at the island's northeastern tip, to wild roses and bluffs of Siasconset, to the inland moors and the lovely beaches of western Madaket, which means 'sandy soil at the end of the land,' Nantucket is like no other place.

101 Purple hydrangea match the trim of this old Victorian cottage – known as a Vineyard gingerbread house – in Oak Bluffs. Initially established as a Methodist religious retreat in the 1800s, the tents at Oak Bluffs were replaced by the houses to provide more comfort.

102-103 The protected harbor at Vineyard Haven, with its ferry terminal and breakwater, dominates this aerial view of Martha's Vineyard's largest port of entry.

104 *The Colonial Inn and Shops in fast-growing
but historic Edgartown provides fine dining, fine
shopping and shelter for the Vineyard's many
visitors.*

105 *Distinguished by the Edgartown Harbor
Lighthouse, the town is considered one of the
yachting capitals of the East Coast. The many
elegant mansions of Edgartown date from
whaling days, when ships crowded the harbor
and island boys sought their fortunes on the high
seas.*

106-107 *A nautical scene in Menemsha blends
whale, flukes and lobster traps with weathered
boats. An authentic fishing village in the
Vineyard's west end, Menemsha is home to many
descendants of the island's first colonial
inhabitants.*

108-109 *The distinctive red cliffs of Gay Head on
the westernmost point of Martha's Vineyard rise
150 feet above the shore.*

110 The graceful 108-foot topsail schooner
Shenandoah anchors in Naushon Island's
Tarpaulin Cove for the night, before its return
cruise across the Sound to Vineyard Haven.
Privately owned Naushon Island is the largest of
the Elizabeth Islands, a chain of 16 small islands
stretching southwest from Woods Hole.

111 A scallop fisherman displays his catch on
Succonnessett Island, one of the Elizabeth
Islands' smallest. The island chain represents the
town of Gosnold, named for the English explorer
Bartholomew Gosnold, who visited here in 1602.

112 A passenger ferry steams into Nantucket
Harbor. Visitors off the boat are treated to the
nineteenth-century village of Nantucket Center,
with its cobblestoned streets, stately mansions,
and rose-covered picket fences.

113 Built by whaling merchant Joseph Starbuck for his three sons, the 'Three Bricks' along Nantucket's Main Street represent the wealth and elegance of the island during its whaling days.

114-115 Moonlight and the glow from waterfront inns and cottages illuminate Nantucket at night. While 'the grey Lady' has her share of hopping night spots and bustling daytime activity, islanders and visitors alike can always find calm moments to enjoy her lovely charm.

116 One of the island's finest shops, the Lion's
Paw in Nantucket Center is bedecked with lights
at Christmas time. Nantucket at Christmas is an
enchanting time, when shops offer music and hot
cider, the trees are lit and carolers fill the streets
with holiday music for the annual Christmas Stroll.

117 Whimsical lawn whirligigs and other craft and
specialty items can be had at this shop on
Straight Wharf on Nantucket's waterfront.

118 *A gaggle of geese makes its way along the road in island mist. Rural Nantucket takes on an ethereal quality in the fog, when the pace slows down and it's easy to imagine the island as it was a century ago.*

119 In the casual and comfortable style that
prevails on Nantucket, a weary traveler relaxes on
the sunporch of a country inn.

120 A couple of islanders clam in Nantucket's mudflats. With a little hard work and a license, shellfishing on Nantucket can yield a variety of delectable treasures.

121 Festive red cranberries and a deep blue sky color an autumn day as bog workers wet-harvest the berries on Nantucket. The island's two major cranberry bogs, cultivated since 1865, are the world's largest.

122-123 Nantucket's moors and marshes harbor abundant wildlife, from marsh hawks and egrets to rabbits and deer.

124 Garden flowers, weathered shingles and a white picket fence add quaintness to a cheery social scene at a summer home in Siasconset, Nantucket's easternmost village.

125 An arched trellis frames the entrance to Nantucket's elegant Chanticleer Inn, a fine and formal restaurant in 'Sconset.

126-127 Nantucket's Smith Point is crowded with surfcasters at sunset. Bass and bluefish are the most common prizes from the shore.